Granny's House

My Southern Childhood

Ashlyne K. Reid

ISBN-13: 978-0-692-99718-5

Dedication

This book is dedicated to my granny, an amazing woman of God. She inspired me to dream bigger than myself and instilled an unshakeable confidence that I can be anything I put my mind to. I will always remember the songs you sung, the smell of your cooking, and your zeal for the Lord. It is because of the sacrifices you made, the example you set and the prophetic words you spoke over me that I am who I am today. You were truly the epitome of a Proverb 31 woman!

"She is clothes with strength and dignity, and she laughs without fear of the future. When she speaks, her words are wise, and she gives instructions with kindness. She carefully watches everything in her household and suffers nothing from laziness. Her children stand and bless her. Her husband praises her; There are many virtuous and capable women in the world, but you surpass them all!"

– Proverbs 31: 25-29

GRANNY'S HOUSE

Contents

Acknowledgments

Photography by Tyrone Sessom

Design Concepts by Trashod Jolly

Written and Created by Ashlyne Reid

Inspired by Granny

Family Memories

~ One day we will see
each other again ~

Granny's House

Granny's house had it all: laughter, fun, food, and even drama! The memories made there will never be forgotten. The smell of vinegar cooking for her famous sauce, sitting in the kitchen as she meal-prepped for a catering order. She taught me the basics, secrets for deep rich favors and how to fix a broken gravy. She had an undeniable passion for food and cooking. It was here that the foundation for my love of Southern cooking began.

From age 7 to 17, I went to Granny's house almost every single day. I remember the sleepovers with cousins, my yearly birthday pool parties, and nightly dinners most nights because my mom knew her strengths and weaknesses. For me, it was basically a second home. As I grew older, I would sit in the kitchen to watch her make dish after dish, day after day. She had an undeniable passion for food. She created a dinner table fit for kings, and every night we sat down as a family, recited grace, and ate her delicious meals.

It is my desire for the world to experience the same amazing dishes and flavor that I had growing up. Therefore, I hope these recipes will find their way onto your stove, into your stomach, and the memories of the rich flavors etched in your heart the way my southern childhood is etched in mine.

Appetizers and Potluck Winners

The beginning of a meal is just as important as the meal itself. Appetizers and potluck winners are a sample of delicious dishes that can be great meal starters or party pleasers. As a working professional, I have added a few short cuts to make these dishes semi- homemade but have that Southern "scratch-made "flavor.

Apple Butter Stuffed Baked Brie

1 frozen puff pastry

1 small wheel of brie

2 teaspoons apple butter

1 egg

½ cup pecans (optional)

---

1. Preheat the oven to 350°F and allow the puff pastry to defrost on a flat surface.
2. Cut the brie in half so you have 2 circles, and place ½ of the cheese on top of the pastry.
3. Spread 2 teaspoons of apple butter and pecans on the cheese circle. Layer the other piece of cheese on top.
4. Carefully fold the puff pastry over the cheese, pinch pastry together at the top to completely cover.
5. Beat the egg with a little water, and brush over the dough.
6. Bake in the over from 20-30 minutes or until golden brown.

Serve with crackers, apple slices, and crusty bread.

Personal preference: Remove the rind from the top and bottom of the Brie.

Crock-Pot BBQ Meatballs

2 bags frozen pre-cooked meatballs

1 bottle hickory & brown sugar BBQ sauce

1 bottle Kraft's Original BBQ sauce

½ cup dark brown sugar

1 teaspoon red pepper flakes

1. In a large crock-pot, combine frozen meatballs and BBQ sauces.
2. Cook on low for 6 hours.
3. After 4 hours, stir in the brown sugar and red pepper flakes.
4. Cook for an additional 2 hours, until sugar has melted and meatballs are heated throughout.

Mom's Crab Pasta Salad

1 box rotini noodles

1 cup fresh broccoli

1 cucumber

2 Roma tomatoes, diced

1 (8-ounce) pack imitation crab meat

1 cup zesty Italian dressing

½ cup mayonnaise

2 teaspoons salt

3 teaspoon ground black pepper

2 teaspoons garlic powder

½ red onion (optional)

1. Cook pasta according to the directions on the box, rinse and set aside.
2. Blanch the broccoli in boiling water for 3-5 minutes and drain.
3. Dice the cucumber, tomatoes, and onion into small pieces and shred the crab meat.
4. In the bottom of a large bowl combine the dressing, mayonnaise and seasonings.
5. Add pasta, crab, and vegetables to the mayonnaise mixture and toss until well combined.

Refrigerate the salad for at least 1 hour (overnight is best) to let the flavors meld.

Granny's Plum Jelly

8-10 red ripe plums

4 cups water

1 pack powdered fruit pectin

2 tablespoon lemon juice

3 cups white sugar

---

1. Wash and remove pits from the plums, place them in a large stockpot, and cover the plums with water.

2. Bring plums to a boil, then reduce to a simmer for 30-45 minutes or until soft.

3. Mash up the softened plums with a potato masher and place a thin dishcloth or cheesecloth over a strainer and squeeze out about 4-5 cups of juice.

4. Put the plum juice back into a smaller pot, mix in the fruit pectin, lemon juice, and sugar. Simmer for 30 minutes.

5. Pour mixture into glass jars and leave out to set.

6. The jelly will only take a couple hours to set, but can enjoyed for up to 3 months refrigerated.

Spinach Artichoke Dip

1 (8-ounce) can artichoke hearts

1 cup shredded mozzarella cheese

8 ounces light cream cheese

½ cup grated Parmesan cheese

3 cloves garlic, minced

2 teaspoons kosher or finely cracked sea salt

2 teaspoons ground black pepper

2 teaspoons garlic powder

2 (16-ounce) bags frozen spinach

grated Parmesan cheese to garnish

1. Drain artichoke hearts. Roughly chop and place into the crock-pot.
2. Add the cheeses and seasonings into the crock-pot and stir.
3. Defrost the frozen spinach in the microwave, and drain excess liquid.
4. Meanwhile, mince the garlic and add to a sauté pan with oil and brown slightly.
5. Turn pan off, then mix spinach into the garlic.
6. Pour spinach mixture into the crock-pot and stir.
7. Cook mixture on low for 4 hours. Stir occasionally.
8. Add a handful of Parmesan cheese to the top before transporting or 20 minutes before serving.

Serve with toasted pita bread or tortilla chips.

Parmesan-Stuffed Mushrooms

15 whole white button mushrooms

3 tablespoons grapeseed or olive oil

2 tablespoons unsalted butter

1 shallot

1 teaspoon minced garlic

½ cup plain breadcrumbs

¼ cup grated Parmesan cheese

2 teaspoons finely-chopped fresh parsley

1 teaspoon finely-chopped fresh thyme

1 teaspoon garlic powder

1 teaspoon ground black pepper

1 teaspoon red pepper flakes

1. Clean mushrooms with damp paper towel and carefully remove stems.

2. Arrange mushrooms, empty side up, on a baking sheet and drizzle with oil. Bake mushrooms for 10 minutes at 300°F or until partially cooked.

3. In a small pan, melt the butter and sauteé the shallots, garlic, chopped mushroom stems, and breadcrumbs for 3-5 minutes until breadcrumbs begin to toast slightly.

4. In a separate bowl, combine cheese and finely chopped herbs. Add breadcrumb mixture to the herbs and cheese to make the stuffing.

5. Season your stuffing with the garlic powder, pepper and red pepper flakes. Stuff mushrooms generously and drizzle with more oil. Bake in the oven for another 15-20 minutes until golden brown on the top.

Guac De Monterrey

2 ripe avocados

1 lime, juiced

½ cup diced Roma tomato

¼ cup pickled jalapeños

¼ cup pickled jalapeño juice

3 teaspoons cilantro

½ teaspoon salt

½ teaspoon pepper

---

1. Cut avocados in half, twist open, and remove the pit.
2. Scoop the inner avocado flesh into a large bowl, squeeze in lime juice (remove any seeds), then roughly mash with a fork.
3. Dice the tomatoes, pickled jalapeños and jalapeño juice and mix in with the avocado.
4. Roughly chop the cilantro and add it with salt and pepper to the mixture, and mix to distribute all the ingredients evenly.

Serve with warmed tortilla chips for an amazing appetizer!

Breakfast at Granny's House

Early mornings, the smell of bacon and pancakes filled the air. Rattling pots and pans move over the gas flame, a table set with bacon, sausage, eggs and a never-ending pot of sweet grits. Golden crispy pancakes stacked high. Just when you thought the last pancake was gone, a fresh new stack was set down in the middle of the table. These are my Saturday morning memories!

Granny's "Deep Fried" Pancakes

2 cups all-purpose flour

1 teaspoon baking soda

2 teaspoons baking powder

2 tablespoons sugar

1 teaspoon salt

2 large eggs

2 cups buttermilk

1 teaspoon vanilla extract

4 tablespoons unsalted butter, melted

½ cup canola oil

1. Preheat an oven to 250°F. To keep pancakes warm and crispy while cooking, you can transfer finished pancakes to an oven-proof dish in the oven.
2. Combine all dry ingredients together (flour, baking soda, baking powder, sugar, and salt).
3. In another bowl whisk together eggs, buttermilk, vanilla extract, and cooled melted butter.
4. Heat oil in a shallow frying pan.
5. Slowly combine the flour into the egg mixture until a thin no-lump consistency forms.
6. Pour ½ cup of batter into the oil, and cook for 1-2 minutes on each side, or until golden brown edges form. The oil should be the height of the pancake but not on top of the pancake.

Mini Omelet Muffins

½ zucchini

½ small yellow onion

1 handful of fresh spinach

1 teaspoon minced garlic

2 teaspoons grapeseed or olive oil

7 large eggs

1 teaspoon ground black pepper

1 teaspoon kosher or finely cracked sea salt

2 teaspoons garlic powder

¼ cup water

---

1. Preheat your oven to 375°F.
2. Chop all veggies into a small dice – each muffin only needs 2 teaspoons of veggies.
3. On medium heat, add the oil into a skillet and add the onions and zucchini, and sauté for 4-5 minutes, next add the minced garlic and spinach and cook until spinach has wilted down. Add the garlic powder, salt and pepper to the filing mixture.
4. Remove skillet from the heat and let filling cool for 3-5 minutes.
5. In a large bowl add the eggs, remaining seasoning and water. Whisk eggs for 2-3 minutes until blended and a little frothy.
6. Spoon 2 teaspoons of cooled filling into each hole in the muffin tin and carefully spoon the egg mixture into the muffin tin so that each are ¾ full.
7. Bake in the oven for 12-15 minutes, or until the eggs are set.

Sweet Grits

2 cups water

2 cups whole milk

2 cups instant grits

½ cup sugar

1 teaspoon kosher or finely cracked sea salt

½ stick unsalted butter

1. Bring water, milk and butter to a simmer.
2. Add in grits and stir for 1 – 2 minutes to prevent lumps from forming.
3. Once the grits come back to a simmer, add sugar and salt.
4. Continue to stir the grits every 2 minutes to prevent scorching the bottom.
5. Once grits have become a creamy thicken mixture, pour into a large bowl to serve.

Although these are instant grits, in order to get a creamier texture, they will need to cook between 15-20 minutes.

Country Ham, Egg, and Cheese Scones

6 pieces of cooked country ham

6 eggs, scrambled

Cheese Scones

2 cups all-purpose flour

1 tablespoon baking powder

1 teaspoon salt

1 teaspoon ground black pepper

4 sticks butter

3oz gouda cheese

3 eggs

¾ cup whole milk or cream

---

1. Mix together flour, baking powder, salt and pepper in a large bowl or food processor.
2. Cut the butter into small cubes and then mix into the flour mixture with a fork or pulse in the food processor until it's crumbly.
3. Cut the cheese into small pieces and mix into the flour mixture.
4. In another bowl combine the eggs and milk and slowly fold milk and egg mixture into the flour and cheese. Combine until the dough comes together forming a ball.
5. Flour a cutting board and knead the dough 5-10 times, flatten out into a 2-inch thick rectangle. Cut the dough using a biscuit cutter and place on a ungreased cookie sheet.
6. Bake in oven for 25 minutes or until golden brown.

Cut scones open and fill with country ham and eggs to make delicious breakfast sandwiches!

Red-Eye Gravy

2 teaspoon canola oil

3 slices country ham

2 cups prepared coffee

½ cup water

1 teaspoon ground black pepper

---

1. Heat oil in a large non-stick pan and add country ham pieces.

2. Cook the ham until crispy on both sides (6-8 minutes per side).

3. Remove the ham and add coffee to deglaze the pan: that means scrape up the pieces of crispy ham bits. Add water and black pepper to the pan, and bring back to boil until warmed through.

4. Add ham back into gravy and serve.

Warm Apple-Cinnamon Oatmeal

1 Granny Smith apple

1 tablespoon unsalted butter

½ cup brown sugar

2 teaspoons salt

3 cups whole milk

3 cups old-fashioned oats

2 teaspoons vanilla extract

2 teaspoons ground cinnamon

chopped walnuts (optional)

1. Wash and peel the apple, then chop it into a small dice.
2. Combine apple, butter, sugar, and salt in a medium saucepan. Cook on low to slowly soften and caramelize the apple for about 8-10 minutes or until the apples soften and turn a golden brown, and the sauce is bubbling.
3. Slowly pour in the milk, and heat to a slight simmer.
4. Add oats, vanilla and cinnamon to the milk mixture. Stir constantly for 10-15 minutes, until it has thickened to the oatmeal consistency you desire.
5. Turn heat off and serve warm with fresh apples or walnuts on top.

Acai Fruit Breakfast Bowl

4 ounces frozen acai

½ cup granola

2 tablespoons creamy almond butter

1 banana, sliced

½ cup blueberries

½ cup apple slices

1. Remove frozen acai and allow it to defrost for 20 minutes or blend until a slushy texture.
2. In a small bowl, put in the granola on the bottom.
3. Top with defrosted acai, then add a layer of almond butter.
4. Cut banana into thin slices and layer the top the bowl with the fruit and berries.

This will almost be like a parfait in which you layer the different ingredients. To mix it up, add any fruit that you love or that is in season.

Traditionally Southern Entrees and Sides

For most of my life, Granny's house was basically my second home. Either a 5-minute walk or 2-minute bike ride down the dirt path. Year-round access to amazing home cooked meals was something I took for granted. Granny had a natural, God-given gift for cooking traditional Southern meals. This section contains 80% of the dishes I grew up eating on a daily basis. Some dishes are more involved than others, but each dish, when made with love, will create lasting memories.

Oven-Baked Chicken

1 whole chicken (5- to 7-pounds, cut into 8 pieces)

2 tablespoons canola or olive oil

4 teaspoons salt (½ for chicken, ½ for rub)

2 teaspoons ground black pepper (½ for chicken, ½ for rub)

4 teaspoons garlic powder (½ for chicken, ½ for rub)

¾ stick unsalted butter (at room temperature)

4 cloves garlic

2 teaspoons paprika

1 teaspoon ground cumin

1. Preheat oven to 400°F.
2. Wash chicken pieces and pat dry with a paper towel.
3. Brush chicken pieces with oil and season with half the salt, half the pepper and half the garlic powder.
4. Mix together butter, garlic and other seasonings to make a pasty rub.
5. Rub the butter paste on the chicken skins.
6. Place in a shallow cooking dish and cover with foil.
7. Bake for 20 minutes. Remove foil and rotate pan.
8. Bake for an additional 30 – 40 minutes until golden brown and thermometer inserted in the thickest part of a thigh reads 165°F.
9. Allow chicken to rest for 10 minutes before slicing, to keep juices from running out.

Stew Beef

3 tablespoons grapeseed or olive oil

1 pot roast (3 pounds)

2 teaspoons salt

4 teaspoons ground black pepper

3 teaspoons garlic powder

1 onion

4 red-skinned potatoes

1 cup white mushrooms

¼ cup soy sauce

¼ cup Worcestershire sauce

2 tablespoons corn starch

1. Heat oil in a large skillet on medium high and season pot roast with salt, pepper, and garlic powder.

2. Brown all sides of the meat in the hot pan and then place into a large crock-pot. Chop the onions, potatoes, and mushrooms in large chunks and add to the crock-pot.

3. Cover the meat and vegetables in the soy sauce and Worcestershire sauce and 1 cup of water on high for 4-6 hours or until tender.

4. Remove roast, cut into large chunks and set aside. In a small dish, mix together cornstarch and ½ cup of liquid from the crock-pot until smooth, then stir into the rest of the liquid in the crock.

5. Add the meat back into the crockpot and cook for an additional 30 minutes until thickened.

Sage Rubbed Pork Loin

1 pork tenderloin (1.5 – 2 pounds)

1 tablespoon ground black pepper

2 tablespoons rubbed sage

2 tablespoons garlic powder

½ teaspoon red pepper flakes

½ teaspoon kosher salt

3 tablespoons grapeseed or olive oil

---

1. Preheat your oven to 375°F. Wash and trim any excess fat from the pork tenderloin and then pat dry with a paper towel.

2. Mix dry seasonings together and sprinkle all over the tenderloin, making sure to rub and press them into the meat.

3. Preheat a skillet (preferably oven-safe) with oil for 1-2 minutes until the oil is hot enough to get a good sizzle. Cook each side for 2-3 minutes until a nice brown sear and crust is formed.

4. Place the oven-safe skillet into the oven, or transfer tenderloin onto a roasting pan for further cooking.

5. Bake tenderloin in the oven for 1 hour, or until internal temperature reaches 160°F.

6. Take tenderloin out of the oven and let rest 10-15 minutes. Slice tenderloin into medallion sized pieces and serve.

Citrus-Glazed Salmon

4 fillets of fresh salmon

3 tablespoons grapeseed or olive oil

2 teaspoons salt

1 teaspoon ground black pepper

½ cup brown sugar

2 limes

2 lemons

2 teaspoons garlic powder

1. Wash salmon filets, place on a baking sheet and pat dry with a paper towel. Brush salmon with oil and season with salt and pepper.

2. In a small bowl, mix together the brown sugar, zest from the limes, zest from the lemons, and garlic powder. Generously cover salmon with brown sugar mixture.

3. Let the salmon sit at room temperature for 15-20 minutes until the brown sugar mixture has formed a wet crust and melted into the filets.

4. Turn oven on low broil and cook salmon for 10-15 minutes until a golden crust has formed. Serve immediately

Smothered Salisbury Steak

8 cubed steaks

2 cups all-purpose flour

¼ cup + 1 tablespoon corn starch

1 teaspoon ground cinnamon

1 teaspoon ground nutmeg

3 teaspoons garlic powder

3 teaspoons onion powder

3 teaspoons salt

2 teaspoons ground black pepper

¼ cup canola oil

1 cup chicken stock

1 yellow onion, sliced

1 tablespoon butter

1. Using a meat mallet or rolling pin, pound out thicker pieces of the cubed steak to break down tissue and keep them from being chewy.

2. In a plastic food storage bag or paper bag, mix together flour, ¼ cup cornstarch and seasonings. Add 2 to 3 pieces of meat to the bag and shake to evenly coat.

3. In a large cast iron skillet, heat canola oil on medium heat. Once oil has heated up, brown meat on each side for 5 – 6 minutes until a golden crust forms.

4. Cook meat in batches and then return all pieces to the pan. Turn heat on low and add ½ cup of chicken stock to the pan and cover. Simmer meat on low for an additional 20-30 minutes until cooked through.

5. Remove meat from the pan, add sliced onions, and cook on low until onions are translucent.

6. Add the rest of the chicken stock. In a small bowl, mix a small amount of stock with 1 tablespoon of cornstarch until dissolved, then whisk into the pan. Once thoroughly combined, melt in one teaspoon of butter (optional) to make a savory and rich pan gravy for the steak. Return the meat into the gravy, and serve over rice.

Southern Fried Pork Chops

6-8 thin bone-in pork chops

1 teaspoon salt

2 teaspoons ground black pepper

1 cup all-purpose flour

¼ cup corn starch

3 teaspoons garlic powder

2 teaspoons Cajun seasoning

½ cup canola oil

1. Wash chops and pat dry with a paper towel. Season with salt and pepper.

2. In a brown paper bag or food storage bag, mix together the flour, cornstarch, and the rest of the seasonings. Toss in 2-3 chops at a time and shake to cover, then remove and place on a separate plate.

3. Place the coated pork chops in the fridge for 15-20 mintues after breading to set and help keep an even coating when frying.

4. Heat oil on medium heat for 5 minutes or until the oil bubbles when you put a little flour in it.

5. Cook 2-3 chops at a time to keep the oil from cooling down too much. Cook the chops 7-10 minutes on each side (depending on thickness).

6. Drain excess oil by placing chops on a pile of paper towels once finished cooking.

7. Preheat oven to 300°F and place finished chops on a wire-racked pan to keep warm while frying the others.

8. Serve warm with any of my Southern sides, such as mashed potatoes or cabbage.

Salmon Croquettes

4 tablespoons grapeseed or olive oil

½ Vidalia onion, diced

2 cans pink Alaskan salmon

2 large eggs

6-8 saltine crackers, crushed

1 teaspoon kosher or finely cracked sea salt

2 teaspoons ground black pepper

2 teaspoons Cajun seasoning

1. In a small sauté pan, add 2 teaspoons of oil and diced onion. Cook on low for 10-15 minutes until translucent and soft.

2. In a medium bowl, add salmon, eggs, crushed crackers, seasonings, and cooked onions. Using your hands or spoon, incorporate all ingredients together and form into 6- 8 medium sized patties.

3. Place patties in refrigerator for 15 – 30 minutes until firm.

4. In a large skillet, add remaining 3 tablespoons of oil and cook croquettes for 5-8 minutes on each side, or until a golden-brown crust forms.

5. Drain croquettes on paper towels or cooling rack and serve warm.

Chicken and Noodles

6 chicken thighs

2 teaspoons salt

3 teaspoons ground black pepper

3 tablespoons grapeseed or olive oil

½ Vidalia onion, sliced

2 teaspoons minced garlic

6 cups chicken stock

1 bag no-yolk noodles

2 (8-ounce) cans cream of chicken

2 teaspoons garlic powder

1. Wash and trim excess skin and fat from chicken thighs. Season with salt and 2 teaspoons of black pepper.

2. In a large stockpot, add oil and onions and sauté for 1-2 minutes, add garlic and sauté for 30 seconds.

3. Add chicken thighs skin-side down for 5-7 minutes, until brown, then turn.

4. Cover chicken thighs with stock and let simmer 30-45 minutes, until the thighs are tender and the meat starts to fall apart.

5. Remove chicken from the pan, add the egg noodles and cream of chicken soup to the chicken stock. Cook for about 15 minutes.

6. Meanwhile, pull the meat off of the chicken, discarding the skin and bones.

7. When the egg noodles have cooked, add the shredded chicken back into the pot. Taste the broth before adding salt and then season with the remaining black pepper and garlic powder.

8. Simmer for an additional 15 minutes or until noodles are soft and flavors have a chance to meld.

If you don't want to use cream of chicken, add 2 cups of heavy cream and 3 tablespoons of cornstarch to thicken. You will have a slightly thinner version, and you may need to add more salt later to bring out the same flavor.

Spicy Fried Chicken

1 whole chicken cut into 8 pieces

3 cups buttermilk

¼ cup Texas Pete hot sauce

3 cups self-rising flour

4 teaspoons salt

4 teaspoons ground black pepper

4 teaspoons garlic powder

4 teaspoons onion powder

4-6 cups peanut or canola oil for frying

3 large eggs

1. Wash chicken and place in a large bowl. Cover the chicken with buttermilk and ½ of the hot sauce (2 tablespoons) and let soak for at least 2 hours.

2. In another bowl mix the flour and seasonings together.

3. In a large heavy bottom pot, heat the oil to 375°F.

4. Remove chicken from buttermilk mixture and heavily coat each piece of chicken in the seasoned flour mixture.

5. Whisk together the eggs and rest of hot sauce. Dip floured chicken in egg mixture and back into seasoned flour. Shake off any excess flour and place into the hot oil.

6. Make sure to move pieces around and flip throughout cooking to get an even color. For larger pieces, cook 25-30 minutes and smaller pieces 20-25 minutes. Preheat oven to 300°F and place drained chicken in a slotted pan in the oven to keep warm.

Chicken Pot Pie

2 deep dish pie crusts

¼ cup Yukon gold potatoes, diced small

¼ cup celery, diced small

½ cup onion, diced small

¼ cup green beans, diced small

4 cup carrots, diced small

3 tablespoons unsalted butter

1 teaspoon minced garlic

3 teaspoons cornstarch

1 ½ cup chicken stock

¼ cup heavy cream

1 cup shredded cooked chicken

1 teaspoon ground black pepper

2 teaspoons salt

¼ cup egg wash (1 egg beaten with 2 tablespoon of water)

1. Preheat oven to 350°F.
2. Take one pie crust, and using a fork, poke holes throughout. Precook the crust in the oven while it preheats.
3. Dice all vegetables into small bite sized pieces. In a large skillet heat butter, add the veggies and cook 5-8 minutes or until tender. Add garlic and then sprinkle vegetables with corn starch and stir to coat evenly.
4. Slowly stir in the chicken stock and cream into the vegetable mixture.
5. Add in cooked chicken and seasonings. Continue to cook 3-5 minutes until it begins to thicken.
6. Remove cooked piecrust from the oven and pour in the filling. Add second crust to the top of the pie, make sure to crimp the edges.
7. Cut at least 4 slits in the top of the pie to allow the steam to escape while the pie cooks.
8. Coat the piecrust with egg wash using a small paint brush or spoon.
9. Bake the pie in the oven 30-40 minutes or until crust is golden brown.

Country Style BBQ Ribs

2 racks baby back pork ribs

Rub

½ cup dark brown sugar

3 tablespoons salt

3 tablespoons ground black pepper

3 tablespoons garlic powder

3 tablespoons chili powder

3 tablespoons hot Mexican paprika

1 tablespoon cumin

Sauce

½ cup brown sugar

¼ cup ketchup

¼ cup apple cider vinegar

2 tablespoons maple syrup

2 tablespoons salt

3 tablespoons ground black pepper

3 tablespoons garlic powder

2 tablespoons red chili flakes

1. Preheat oven to 300°F. Wash and trim excess fat off ribs. It's also important to remove the thin "silver skin" off the backside of ribs.
2. Combine all the rub ingredients in a bowl until evenly mixed.
3. Get two large pieces of tin foil for each rack and generously massage in the rib rub to all parts of the ribs.
4. Double-wrap ribs in tin foil, place on a large baking sheet, and bake in oven for 3.5 hours.
5. In a small saucepan, combine all ingredients for sauce and cover on low, stirring occasionally. Unwrap ribs and place in baking dish. Liberally cover ribs with sauce, saving extra sauce for table topping.
6. Increase oven temperature to 400°F and cook the ribs an additional 20-30 minutes, until caramelized.

Gloria's Potato Salad

1 bag Yukon gold potatoes (5 pounds)

6 large eggs

¼ cup sugar

2 teaspoons salt

2 teaspoons ground black pepper

1 cup mayonnaise

2 teaspoons yellow mustard

1 cup sweet pickle relish

---

1. Wash your potatoes, place in a large stockpot, and cover with water. Bring water to a boil and cook potatoes for 20-30 minutes or until tender.

2. Drain potatoes and run cold water over to stop cooking. Peel skins off, dice into large cubes, and place into a large bowl.

3. Meanwhile in another small pot, cover your eggs with cold water and bring to a boil. Boil eggs for 3-4 minutes and then turn heat off and cover until you have finished peeling your potatoes.

4. Peel the boiled eggs, roughly chop, and add eggs to potatoes.

5. Season potatoes and eggs with sugar, salt and pepper. Finally mix in the mayonnaise, mustard and relish until you get the consistency you like.

6. Refrigerate the salad for at least 1-2 hours to let the flavor meld and serve!

Tip: If you stick a fork into the boiled potatoes and it slides right off, you know it's done.

Spicy Garlic Green Beans

3 tablespoons grapeseed or olive oil

1 tablespoon unsalted butter

½ Vidalia onion

1 tablespoon minced garlic

1 (16-ounce) bag frozen whole green beans

2 teaspoons ground black pepper

3 teaspoons kosher or finely cracked sea salt

4 teaspoons garlic powder

¼ cup chicken stock

1/2 teaspoon red pepper flakes (optional)

---

1. On medium heat, melt the oil and butter together. Add red pepper flakes into oil and butter for 30 seconds to marinate the oil.

2. Add onions and sauté for 3-5 minutes. Add garlic and stir for 30 seconds until there is a nutty fragrance.

3. If using frozen green beans, microwave the green beans for 3-4 minutes, just to defrost the beans. If using fresh green beans, blanch the beans in salted boiling water for 5 minutes.

4. Add green beans to sautéed onions and garlic. Add seasonings and mix together. Finally, add the chicken stock then cover your skillet to let the green beans steam for 5-10 minutes, until tender.

If you skip step 3, your green beans will take longer to soften and will be crunchier.

Roasted Rosemary Potatoes

1 bag of red skinned potatoes (3 pounds)

3 tablespoons grapeseed or olive oil

1 tablespoon minced garlic

1 teaspoon ground black pepper

1 teaspoon kosher or finely cracked sea salt

2 teaspoons garlic powder

½ teaspoon red pepper flakes (optional)

2 teaspoons dried rosemary

1. Preheat your oven to 400°F.
2. Wash and cut the potatoes into small bite size cubes. Place the potatoes on a foil-lined or nonstick cookie sheet.
3. Make sure that the potatoes are in an even layer with enough space to flip once or twice, and toss in the oil.
4. Add remaining ingredients and toss potatoes to cover.
5. Put the baking sheet on the bottom rack of your oven and bake for 30-45 minutes. Make sure you flip and move the potatoes around every 15 minutes for even browning.
6. Let cool for 3-5 minutes and serve.

Cabbage and Fat Back

6-8 fat back pieces

3 tablespoons grapeseed or olive oil

2 whole green cabbages

1 yellow onion

1 green bell peppers

3 tablespoons white sugar

2 teaspoons ground black pepper

2 teaspoons salt

½ teaspoon red pepper flakes

¼ cup apple cider vinegar

½ cup chicken stock

---

1. Be sure to wash or blanch fat back pieces in boiling water to cut down on the saltiness.
2. In a deep stockpot, lay thin slices of fat back and cook in oil until fat is rendered and pieces are hard and crispy.
3. Thinly slice the cabbage, onions and green peppers. Slowly add vegetables to the rendered oil and stir to coat vegetables with the oil. Wait 5 minutes until the first batch of cabbage begins to wilt if you are having a hard time getting it all in the pot.
4. Once all the vegetables are in the pot, add sugar and seasonings, and sauté in oil for 5 minutes. Add in the chicken stock and apple cider vinegar, and turn heat down to low.
5. Allow the cabbage and vegetables to cook down for an additional 45 to 60 minutes, or until your desired tenderness. Traditionally, my granny made this very tender but I prefer a bite in my cabbage.
6. Once cooked down serve with the crispy fat back (if there are any left).

Black Peppered Corn

15 ears sweet white corn

5-6 pieces of bacon or 3 tablespoons bacon drippings

¼ cup sugar

2 teaspoons salt

3 teaspoons ground black pepper

1. Shuck and wash the corn ears (best to use fresh corn from a farmers' market or local garden). For easy shucking, cut the bottom of the corn (stem-end) and slide out of the husk. Carefully cut the kernels off the corn and squeeze as much corn milk as you can into the bowl before discarding the cobs.

2. In a large stockpot, place 5-6 pieces of bacon and slowly render off the fat, being careful not to burn.

3. On low heat, slowly mix in corn, sugar, salt, and pepper. Feel free to add more or less pepper to this dish, but I love the amount of pepper that's in this dish. Cook on low heat for 30 – 45 minutes until it begins to thicken slightly.

4. Serve warm.

In step 2, if you already have bacon drippings from breakfast that works too!

Maggie's Baked Mac & Cheese

1 stick of butter

1 pound elbow macaroni noodles

4 teaspoons salt

4 teaspoons ground black pepper

1 pound sharp cheddar cheese, shredded

1 pound mild cheddar cheese, shredded

5 large eggs

3 cups whole milk

1. Preheat oven to 350°F.

2. Add butter to a large pot of water and bring to a boil. Add macaroni and stir to break up any clumps. Stir again after 2 minutes. Cook macaroni for 8 to 10 minutes until al dente.

3. Drain pasta, but do not rinse. Place pasta back into pot and add salt and pepper. Make sure the surface of the noodles is fully covered in pepper and salt.

4. Mix in ½ of sharp and mild cheese into the warm pasta and stir until it begins to melt.

5. Pour ½ of pasta mixture into a deep casserole dish or short aluminum pan and layer with sharp cheese.

6. Layer the rest of the pasta on top of cheese and set aside. Whisk eggs and milk together.

7. Pour milk & egg mixture over pasta. It should be enough to fill the pan ¾ of the way full. Cover the rest of the pasta with the remaining shredded mild cheese.

8. Place dish into the oven and bake for 30 – 40 minutes, until firm and no liquids are visible.

Sautéed Kale with Bacon

1 tablespoon grapeseed or olive oil

2 slices bacon

½ Vidalia onion

1 tablespoon minced garlic

1 box chicken stock

2 bags prewashed kale

½ teaspoon red pepper flakes

2 teaspoons salt

1 teaspoon ground black pepper

2 teaspoons garlic powder

---

1. Use a large stockpot on medium to heat oil and add bacon until most of the fat is rendered.
2. Remove bacon and add thinly sliced onions. Sauté onions for 2-3 minutes, and add garlic. Add ½ of chicken stock to pot and bring it to a simmer.
3. Add kale in batches, as it will slowly wilt down after the chicken stock steams it. Once all kale is cooking, add in the rest of the seasonings and cover.
4. Stir kale every 15 minutes for 1-2 hours or until tender. As the liquid begins to evaporate, add more stock as needed.

Cinnamon Stewed Apples

2 large Fuji apples

2 lemons

½ cup light brown sugar

¼ cup white sugar

½ teaspoon salt

3 teaspoons cinnamon

---

1. Wash, peel and core the apples.
2. Cut the apples into large slices (they do not have to be even). Place apples in the stockpot.
3. Squeeze lemon juice from the two lemons, removing seeds. Pour juice over the apples. Add the sugars, salt, and cinnamon to the apple mixture and stir.
4. Allow the apples to cook on medium low for 1 hour or until tender.

BBQ Baked Beans

3 bell peppers (1 yellow, 1 red and 1 green)

1 Vidalia onion

2 tablespoons grapeseed or olive oil

2 cups dark brown sugar

2 teaspoons salt

2 teaspoons ground black pepper

3 teaspoons garlic powder

2 teaspoons onion powder

2 teaspoons chili powder

2 teaspoons hot Mexican paprika

4 cans baked beans

4 slices bacon

1. Preheat oven to 400°F.
2. Dice peppers and onion. Heat oil in a pan, and sauté peppers and onion until softened.
3. In a small bowl, combine sugar and spices.
4. Place beans in a deep metal pan. Set aside ½ cup of sugar-spice mix for the top, sprinkle the rest over the beans.
5. Stir in onions and peppers, top with bacon and remaining spice mix.
6. Bake the beans for 20-25 minutes or until bacon is cooked and a golden-brown crust forms.

Caramelized Maple-Candied Yams

1 bag of sweet potatoes (3-5 pounds)

2 tablespoons grapeseed or olive oil

½ stick unsalted butter

½ cup light brown sugar

½ cup white sugar

3 teaspoons cinnamon

2 teaspoons nutmeg

1 teaspoon kosher or finely cracked sea salt

2 tablespoons maple syrup

¼ cup chopped pecans

1. Preheat your oven to 400°F.

2. Wash and place potatoes on a foil-lined or nonstick baking sheet and toss in oil. Put the baking sheet on the bottom rack of your oven and bake for 1.5-2 hours until potatoes are tender.

3. In a small stockpot on medium heat, combine butter, ¼ cup of each sugar, 2 teaspoons of cinnamon, nutmeg, salt, and maple syrup. Cook about 10-12 minutes until it begins to bubble and look similar to a caramel sauce.

4. Combine the rest of the ingredients (¼ cup of each sugar, 1 teaspoon of cinnamon, pecans) in another bowl and stir. Set aside.

5. Allow potatoes to cool slightly, peel and slice length way and arrange in a 9x12 baking dish. Sprinkle dry pecan mix on top of potatoes, then pour butter & sugar mixture over potatoes.

6. Bake for 15-20 minutes, until bubbly and caramelized.

Parmesan Garlic Mashed Potatoes

1 head whole garlic

4 tablespoons grapeseed or olive oil

2 tablespoons kosher or finely cracked sea salt

1 pound baby Yukon gold potatoes

½ cup chicken stock

½ cup heavy cream or whole milk

2 tablespoons unsalted butter

½ cup grated Parmesan cheese

2 teaspoons ground black pepper

2 teaspoons garlic powder

1-2 chopped chives (garnish only)

---

1. Preheat oven to 400°F.

2. Cut head of garlic in half lengthwise and wrap in tin foil with 2 tablespoons of oil. Bake garlic for 30 minutes until golden brown and soft. Scoop out roasted garlic from the paper casings, mash in a small bowl, and set aside.

3. Bring a large pot of water to boil, add 2 tablespoons of salt and potatoes. Cook potatoes for 25- 30 minutes until tender or they easily slide off a fork.

4. In a small saucepan, combine chicken stock, cream, and butter. Bring to a low simmer.

5. Drain potatoes, add the roasted garlic to the pot, and smash together to incorporate. Add ½ of the chicken stock mixture, Parmesan cheese, black pepper, and garlic powder. Stir well.

6. Add the rest of the liquid if necessary if mixture is too thick. Garnish with chives for an elevated flavor.

Roasted Asparagus with Honey Balsamic Glaze

1 cup balsamic vinegar

2 tablespoons honey

1 teaspoon kosher or finely cracked sea salt

2 bunches whole asparagus

¼ cup grapeseed or olive oil

1 tablespoon minced garlic

1 teaspoon ground black pepper

2 teaspoons garlic powder

1. Preheat oven to 400°F.

2. In a small stockpot, combine vinegar and honey and pinch of salt and cook on medium high for 15-20 minutes until sauce has reduced into thin syrup.

3. Meanwhile, wash asparagus, trim woody part of stems, and place on a long cookie sheet. Generously roll in oil, minced garlic, and seasonings, then bake for 15 – 20 minutes, until tender.

4. Placed cooked asparagus on a serving dish and drizzle with the balsamic reduction, and serve.

Thanks "Giblet" Gravy

1 pack raw giblets (found inside of most whole birds)

2 ½ cups water

2 tablespoons unsalted butter

2 teaspoons all-purpose flour

1 to 1 ¼ cups whole milk or chicken stock

1/2 teaspoon kosher or finely cracked sea salt

½ teaspoon ground black pepper

¼ cup chopped mushrooms (optional)

1. Place giblets in the water to and bring to a boil. Lower heat and simmer for 15 – 20 minutes or until cooked through.

2. Remove giblets from water and chop into small pieces.

3. Melt butter in a skillet, add flour and cook until a medium brown color, 3-5 minutes. Slowly whisk in 1 cup milk or chicken stock to the flour/butter mixture, whisking well to prevent lumps .

4. Add in the chopped pieces of giblets, mushrooms, salt and pepper to the mixture as it thickens.

5. If too thick, add ¼ cup of additional milk or chicken stock to thin it out

Tip: For a richer sauce add 2 more tablespoons of butter at the end before serving.

Roasted Pickled Beets

8-10 fresh beets with roots trimmed

4 cups apple cider vinegar

2 cups white sugar

2 teaspoons salt

12 whole cloves

2-3 cinnamon sticks

1 cheesecloth

1. Preheat oven to 400°F.
2. Thoroughly wash beets (they can be very dirty) and wrap 2 – 3 beets together in several tinfoil bundles. Place beet bundles into a large baking dish and bake for 2 hours or until tender.
3. Use disposable gloves during this step or your hands will turn magenta. While still warm, peel or rub skins off of beets and slice into disks or half-moon shapes.
4. In a large stockpot, combine vinegar, sugar, and salt. Heat on low until dissolved. Tie up the cloves and cinnamon into the cheesecloth and steep the spice mixture in the vinegar for 20 to 25 minutes.
5. Prepare jars for canning and fill jar with the sliced beets. Slowly pour vinegar mixture into the jars and seal. Allow beets to marinate in the mixture 48 to 72 hours before eating to allow pickling to take place.

Oven-Roasted Veggies

1 yellow squash, 1" cubes

1 bunch of asparagus, 1" cubes

1 Vidalia onion, 1" cubes

head of broccoli crowns, 1" cubes

3 tablespoons grapeseed or olive oil

½ teaspoon salt

½ teaspoon pepper

1 teaspoon garlic powder

3 teaspoons garlic and herb seasoning mix

1. Preheat the oven to 400°F.
2. Chop all veggies into similar size pieces for consistent roasting time.
3. Coat the veggies in oil and mix with your hands for even coverage. Sprinkle all seasonings over the veggies and mix again with your hands.
4. Bake for 30 minutes, turning the veggies half way through the roasting time.

Collard Greens

¼ cup grapeseed or olive oil

½ yellow onion, sliced

1 tablespoon minced garlic

2-3 smoked turkey necks or wings

4 cups low sodium chicken stock

1 teaspoon red pepper flakes

1 teaspoon sugar

2 teaspoons kosher or finely cracked sea salt

2 (16-ounce) bags fresh collards, washed and chopped

---

1. In a large stockpot, add oil and sauté onions until translucent. Add garlic, turkey, and red pepper flakes to oil, let brown for 1-2 minutes, stirring occasionally.

2. Cover turkey in chicken stock, add the sugar and salt. Let simmer 30 minutes to 1 hour. Remove turkey, shred the meat off the bones, and add meat back to the liquid.

3. Add greens to the pot and cover. Stir occasionally as greens begin to wilt.

4. Greens will need to cook 3 – 4 hours until tender.

Tip: Never let the liquid in your greens boil, as this will cause them to become tough.

Scratch-Made Desserts

Granny did not have much of a sweet tooth. She stuck to mostly fruit and savory foods but when she felt the urge, an apple pie or banana pudding was sure to follow. Many of her desserts were made for large family gatherings such as Thanksgiving, Christmas, Easter, 4th of July and birthdays. Therefore, all of these desserts can be made year round ,so try them out and impress the non sweet tooth in your family.

Scratch-Made Banana Pudding

½ cup sugar

⅓ cup all-purpose flour

1 teaspoon salt

1 cup evaporated milk

1 can sweetened condensed milk

2 cups whole milk

2 eggs yolks

2 teaspoons vanilla extract

2 boxes vanilla-flavored wafer cookies

6-8 ripe bananas

whipped cream (optional)

1. In a medium sized pot, mix together sugar, flour, salt, and milks, heat on high heat until dissolved, then reduce to low.

2. Place egg yolks in a separate bowl, beat well, adding 2 to 3 tablespoons of the warm milk and sugar mixture to temper the eggs.

3. Turn the heat off, add tempered eggs into the milk mixture, and whisk constantly for 7-8 minutes, until a thick custard forms.

4. Strain mixture through a thin sieve into a bowl just in case any of the egg has curdled. Stir in vanilla, and set custard to the side to cool.

5. Now begin to layer ingredients in a deep rectangular dish: first layer the cookies, then a layer of bananas, top with ⅓ of the pudding. Repeat for three layers. Cover the top with cookies.

6. Refrigerate the pudding for 2 to 3 hours, and top with whipped cream if you'd like before serving.

Tip: It is very important that all ingredients be at room temperature to help custard remain creamy.

Peach Ice Cream

6-8 yellow peaches

¼ cup sugar

½ teaspoon salt

1 lemon, juiced

1 can sweetened condensed milk

1 cup whole milk

½ cup heavy cream

1. Peel peaches, cut up and reserve 2 peaches to fold in later. Puree the remaining peaches with the sugar, salt, and lemon juice. Refrigerate peaches and peach puree.
2. In a bowl, combine both milks and cream, and refrigerate for at least 30 minutes.
3. Combine peach puree and peach pieces into the milk mixture.
4. Add mixture to an ice cream maker or put into a dish and freeze overnight.

Apple Pie

10-15 Cripps Pink or Pink Lady apples, peeled and sliced

1 lemon, juiced

1 cup white sugar

1 cup brown sugar

½ teaspoon salt

1 teaspoon nutmeg

2 teaspoons cinnamon

2 deep dish pie crusts

2 tablespoons unsalted butter

1 egg

¼ cup water

---

1. Peel, core and slice the apples and place in a large bowl. Squeeze lemon juice from the lemon over the apples. Add the sugars, salt and spices and combine.

2. Line a medium-length sheet pan with foil to catch any spills and place under the rack that will have the pie.

3. Preheat the oven to 400°F. Prick holes in one crust with a fork and bake for 15 minutes while the oven preheats. Allow the other crust to defrost to use as the top crust.

4. Pour apple mixture into the cooked crust, cover with thin slices of butter.

5. Cover the apples with the second crust and make sure to have some slits in the crust to allow the steam to release. Feel free to get decorative here with the top crust, making a lattice style or any design.

6. Prepare an egg wash by mixing egg with water. Brush the egg wash over the crust and sprinkle top with a little cinnamon and sugar (optional).

7. Bake pie for 30-35 minutes or until golden brown and bubbling.

8. Allow the pie to cool for 15 minutes before serving with ice cream or whipped topping.

Almond Date Bars

½ cup dry roasted almonds

1 cup whole pitted dates

½ cup dried cranberries (no sugar added)

---

1. Place all ingredients in a food processor.
2. Pulse until a slight ball forms, or all ingredients are combined.
3. Press mixture flat on a cookie sheet and chill until firm.
4. Once thoroughly chilled, cut into bars and wrap in plastic wrap or put into snack-sized plastic bags.

You can roll into a log and wrap in plastic wrap, refrigerate and cut into disks.

Southern Beverages

Many hot spring and summer days as a kid were spent outside swimming in the pool, riding bikes, and playing four corners upstairs at Granny's house. When we got thirsty, we could always count on a cold glass of sweet tea or lemonade. For those who did not grow up in the South, I really have no explanation for our sweet tea obsession, but it is real. The secret to any tea dish is to not let the water boil. Take a look at these next few pages to quench your Southern thirst.

Sparkling Iced Green Tea

6 cups water

3 bags green tea

2 bags lemon ginger tea

¼ cup sugar

2 tablespoons honey

2 teaspoons lemon juice

1 bottle sparkling white grape juice

1. In a large pot, heat 6 cups of cold water to a light simmer while steeping tea bags.
2. Once bags have steeped for 10 minutes, remove bags. Add sugar and honey, stirring until dissolved.
3. Add lemon juice, then cool down with ice, or put it in the refrigerator to chill.
4. Before serving, stir in the sparkling white grape juice for a light and fruity sparkle.

Blueberry Mint Lemonade

1 cup sugar

6-8 lemons, juiced

2 cups fresh blueberries

6 cups water

ice cubes

4 mint leaves

1. In a large stockpot, mix together sugar, the juice from the lemons, and whole blueberries.
2. Heat the mixture on medium heat for 10-15 minutes, until the sugar has melted and the blueberries begin to break down.
3. In a large pitcher, combine the mixture with water and ice.
4. Sprinkle in the mint and refrigerate for 30 minutes to let the flavors meld.

Southern Sweet Tea

2 gallons water

6-8 large black tea bags

3 cups white sugar

¼ cup honey

2 lemons, sliced

1. In a large stockpot, pour in the two gallons of water and bring to a boil. Turn the heat down low, add the tea bags, and let it steep 15 minutes.

2. Squeeze excess water from tea bags and discard them. Turn heat off and slowly stir in the sugar and honey until dissolved.

3. Pour tea back into gallon jugs or a pitcher and add lemon slices.

4. Refrigerate for at least 2 hours, and serve over ice.

Never allow the water to boil while the tea bags are in water.

Country Sangria

½ *cup brown sugar*

1 cup blackberries

2 cups blueberries

1 yellow peach, diced (unpeeled)

2 bottles dry red wine (cabernet)

½ *cup bourbon*

½ *cup orange juice*

1 cup lemon-lime soda

---

1. In a medium pot, melt sugar with ½ cup of blackberries and 1 cup of blueberries.
2. In a large pitcher, add peaches, wine, bourbon, orange juice, fruit and sugar mixture, and soda.
3. Stir well. Let sit 2-3 hours in the refrigerator to allow all the flavors to meld before serving over ice.

About the Author

Ashlyne Kelly Reid, CPA, MAC

ASHLYNE REID is the oldest of Granny's 10 grandchildren. She graduated with a Master's degree in Accounting from UNC Chapel Hill and is currently a CPA at a fortune 500 company in Charlotte, NC. In 2015, she began a small catering company called Southern Apron Cooking. She enjoys traveling, spending time with family and of course cooking. Her passion for family, food and the Lord inspired her to author her first cookbook titled "Granny's House: My Southern Childhood".

"Trust in the Lord with all your heart; and do not depend on your own understanding. Seek His will in all you do, and He will show you which path to take."

Proverbs 3: 5-6 (NLT)

I just want to give a special thanks to everyone who has helped me make this dream into a reality. To my family and friends who tested recipes, proofread text, and simply encouraged me. I thank you all from the bottom on my heart.

With love,
Ashlyne

Made in the USA
Middletown, DE
16 June 2021